Mr. Bumbleticker's Birthday

Written by Sandra Iversen ☆ Illustrated by Peter Paul Bajer

"Get up, Mr. Bumbleticker," said the dog.
"It is your birthday.
I have a present for you."

Mr. Bumbleticker got up.

A fish from the cat.
A bone from the dog.
A cake from Mrs. Bumbleticker.

The cat ate the fish.
The dog ate the bone.
Mr. and Mrs. Bumbleticker ate the cake.

"I like my birthday,"
said Mr. Bumbleticker.

"We like your birthday, too,
Mr. Bumbleticker,"
said Mrs. Bumbleticker
and the cat and the dog.